SUPER NATURAL

a colouring book

by Janine Carrington

This book is dedicated
 to all the real life
superheroes that
I know.

Working together I know
we can accomplish our
mission.

The following pages contain 17 superheroes and their sun enhanced natural tendencies.

Grab your crayons, markers, pens, pencils, paint, photoshop pencil crayons, pastels, conte and whatever to help them

SAVE THE WORLD!

A word of warning, the information in this book is not classified so feel free to share with everyone you know Some of these superheroes might be even be someone you recognize. If so, write me and tell me why you think so!

janine.carrington@gmail.com

Super Tip!

Our superheroes enhance their powers by harnessing the light of the sun with their hair. If you want, help show the sun's glow by colouring lightly at the edges of their curls

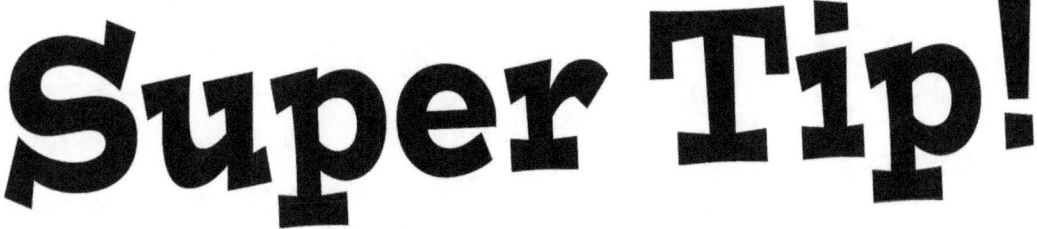

Let's save the world!

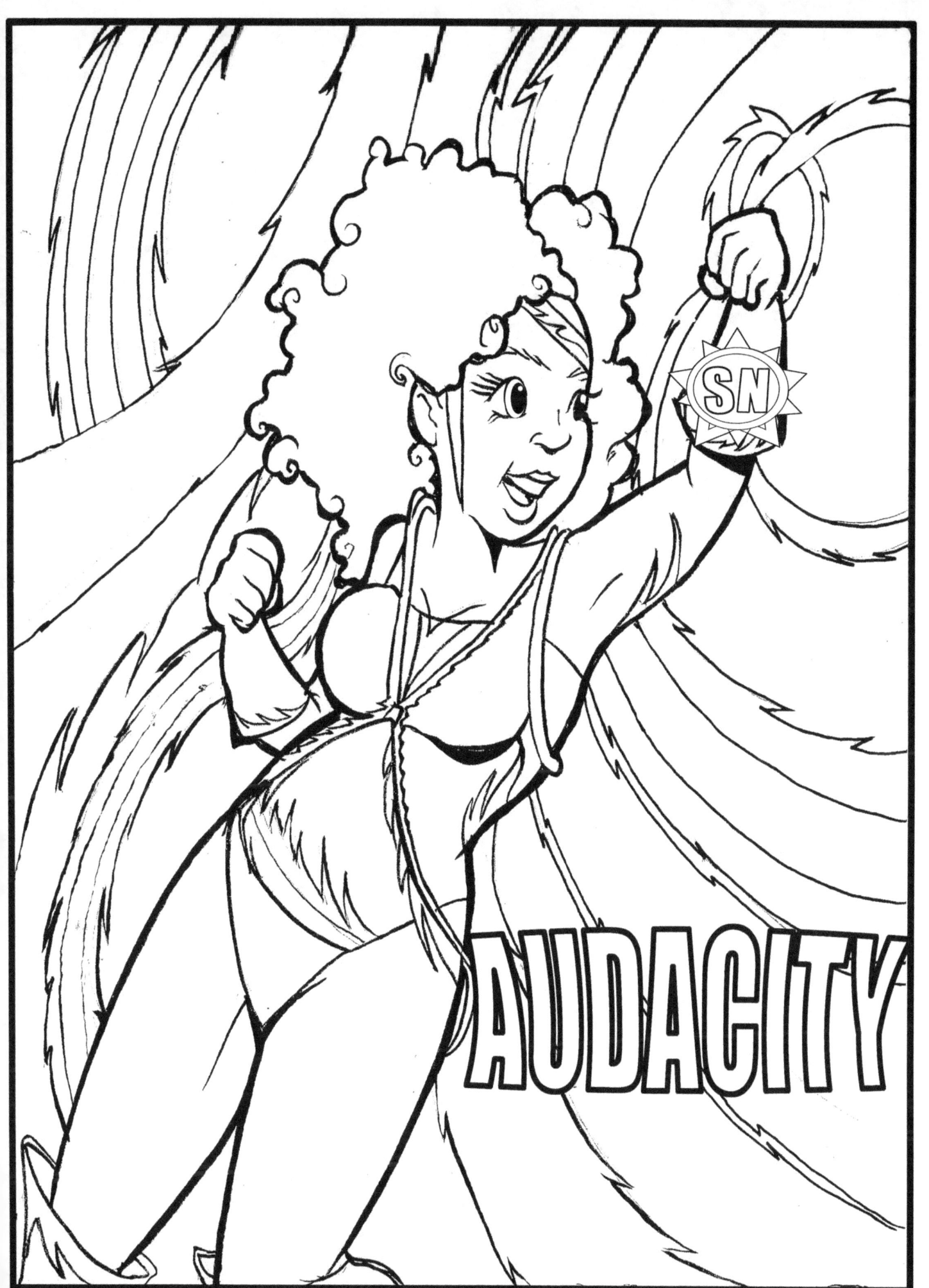

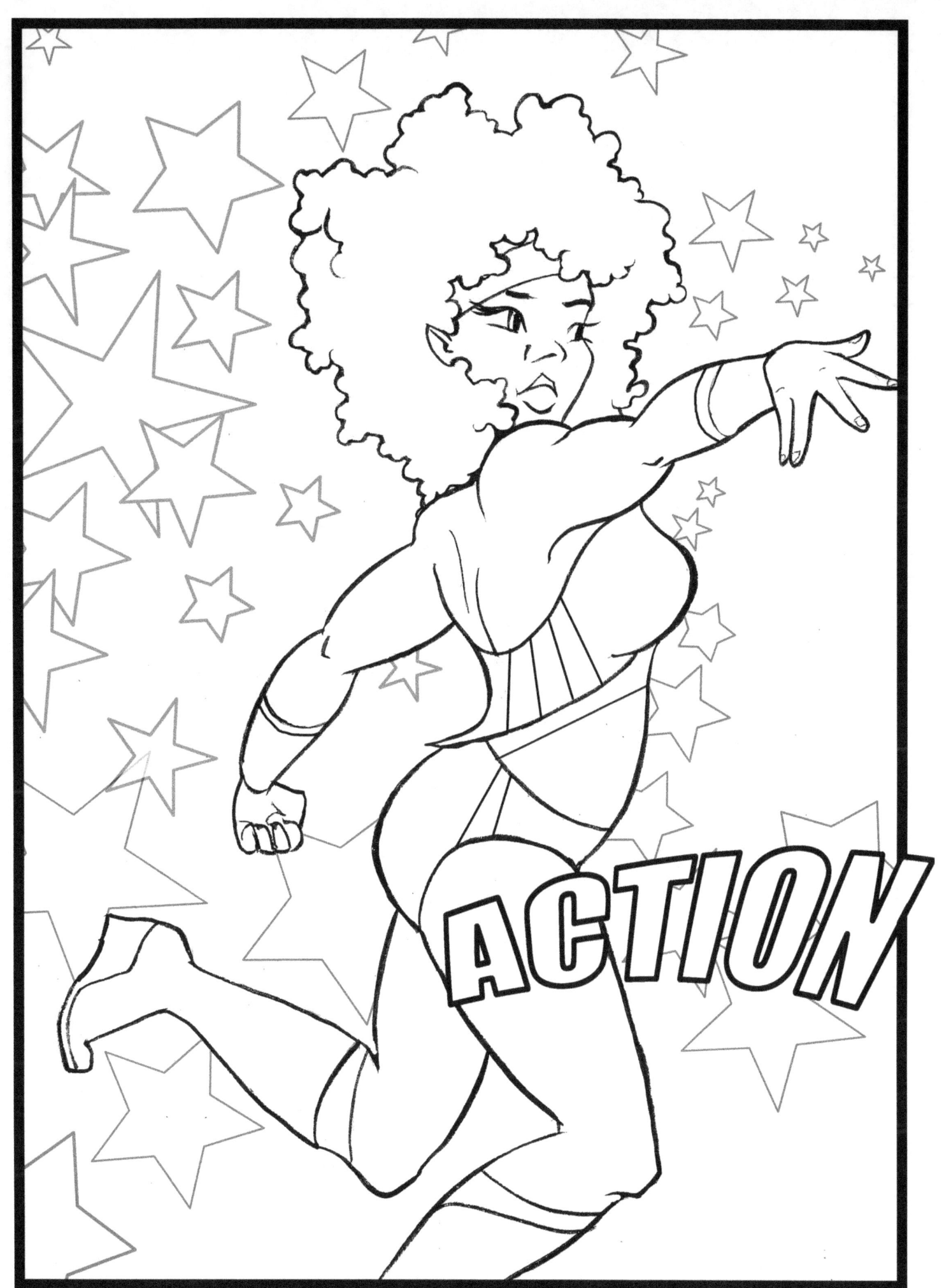

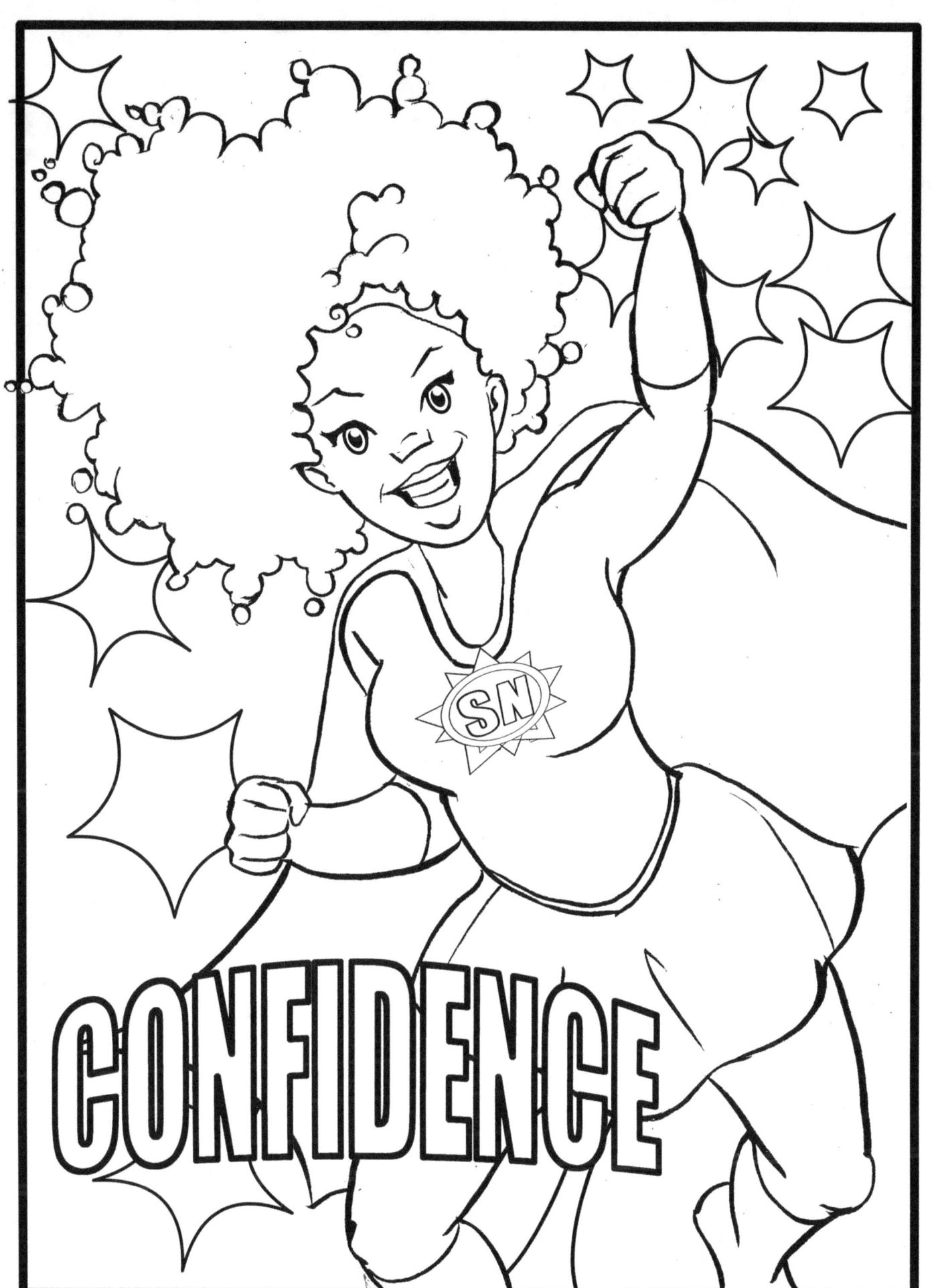

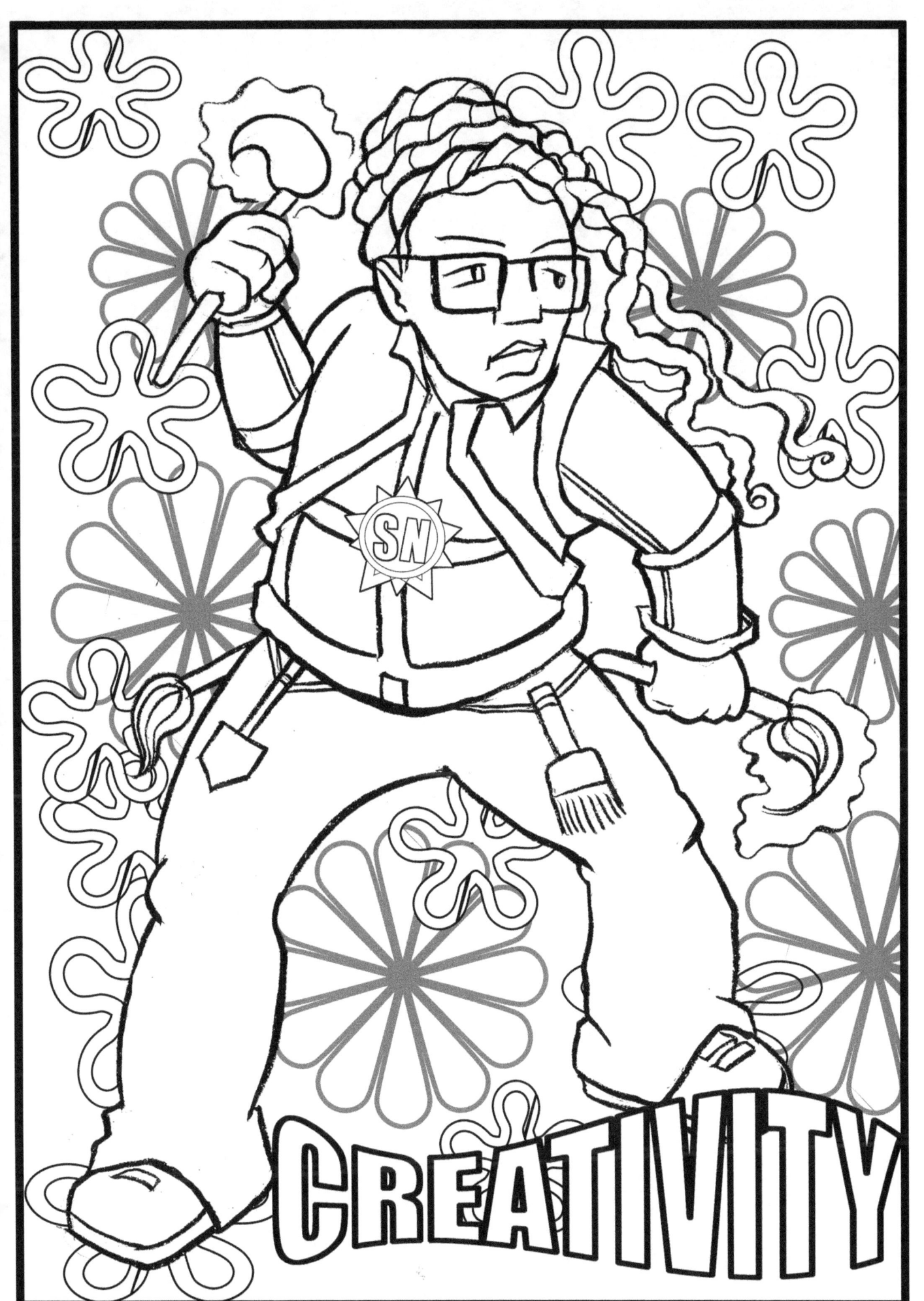

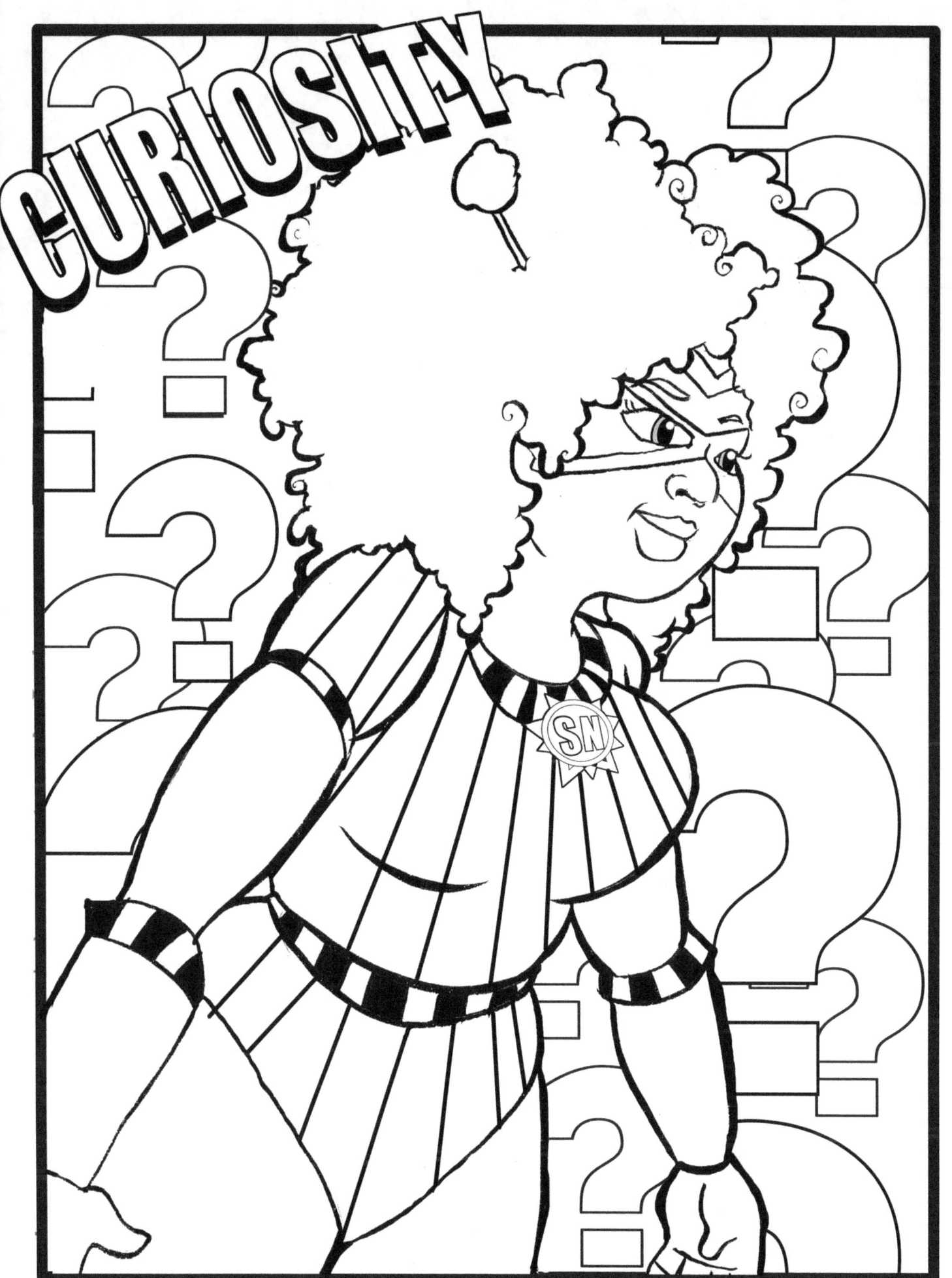

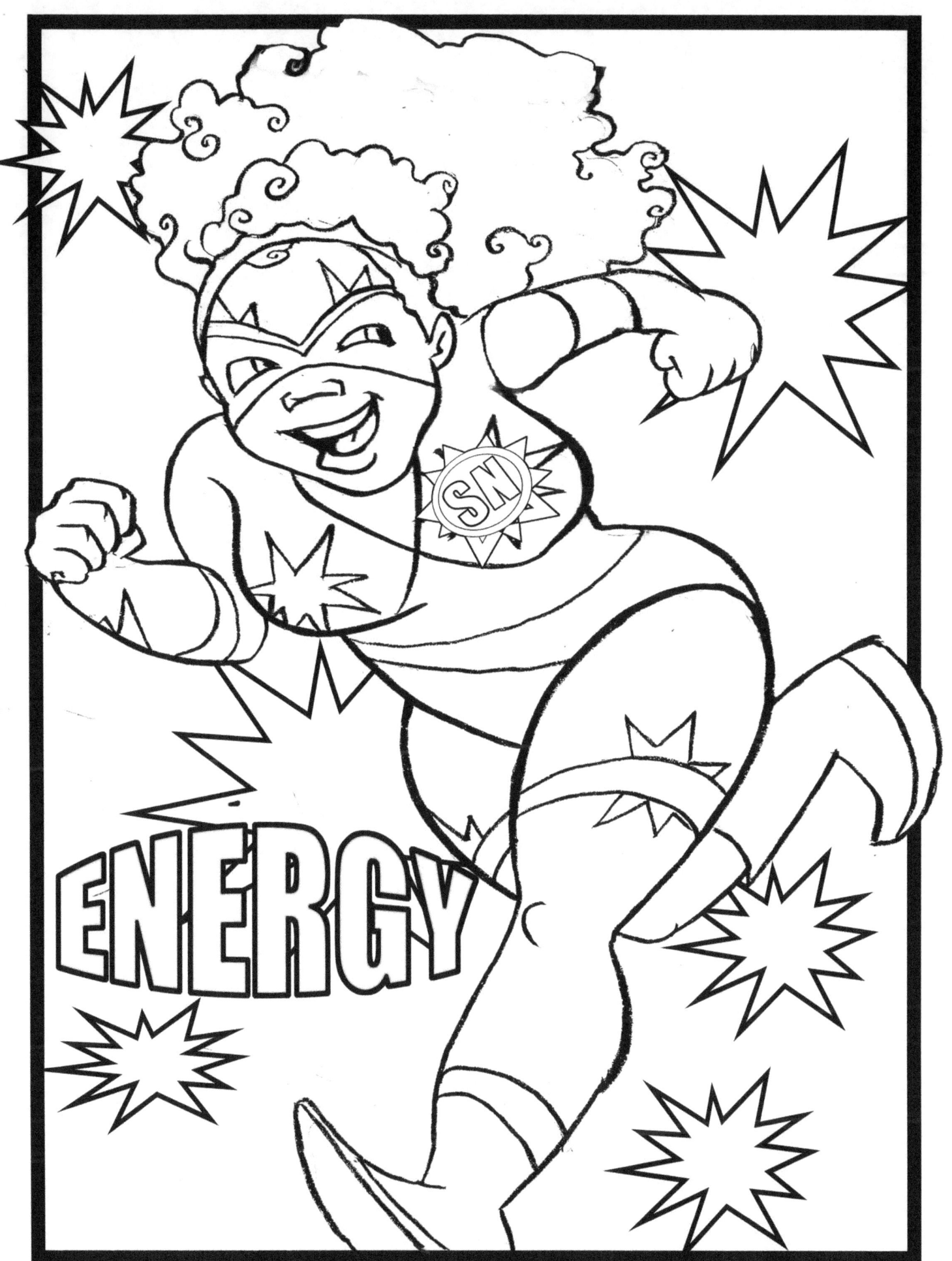

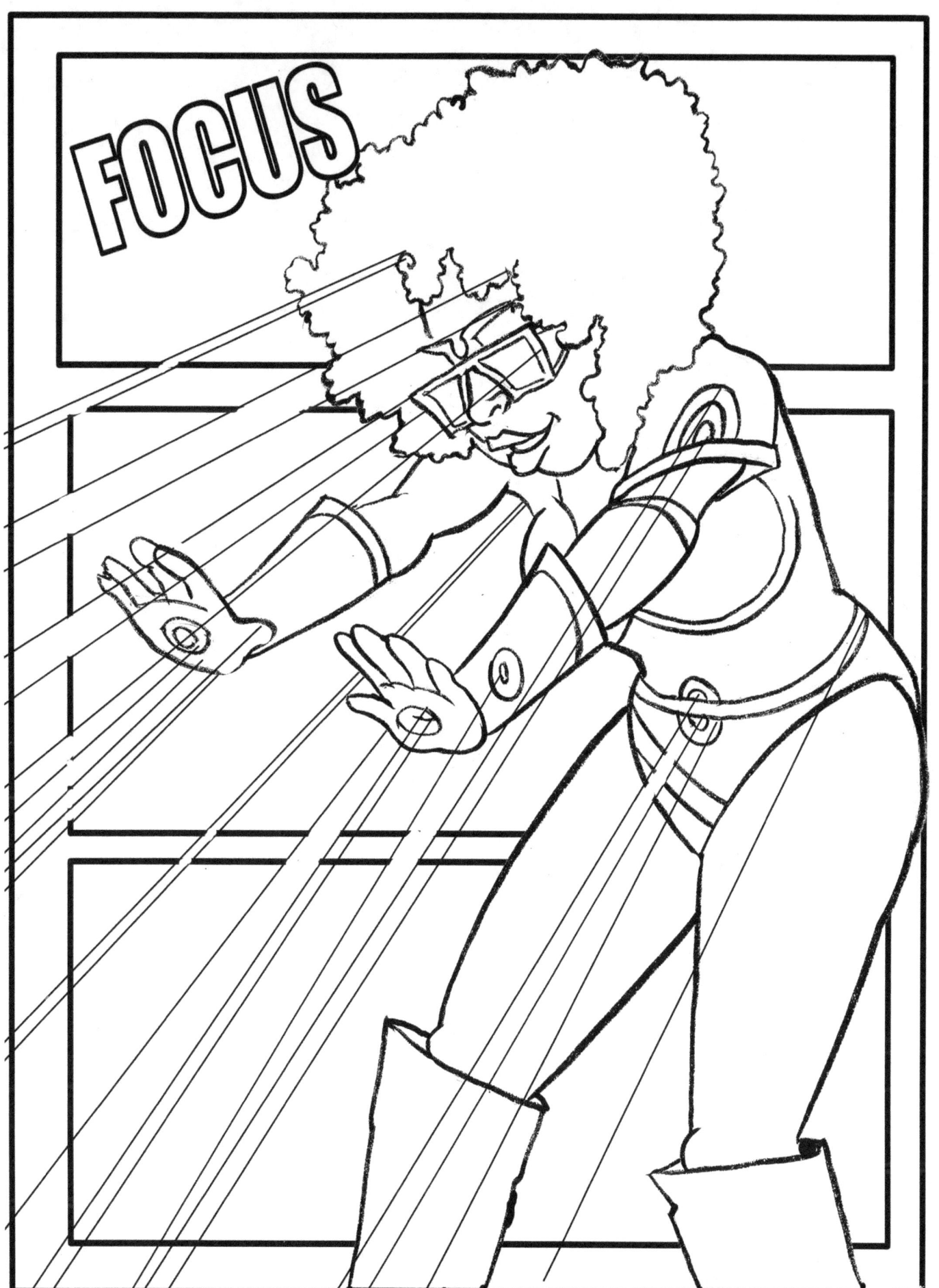

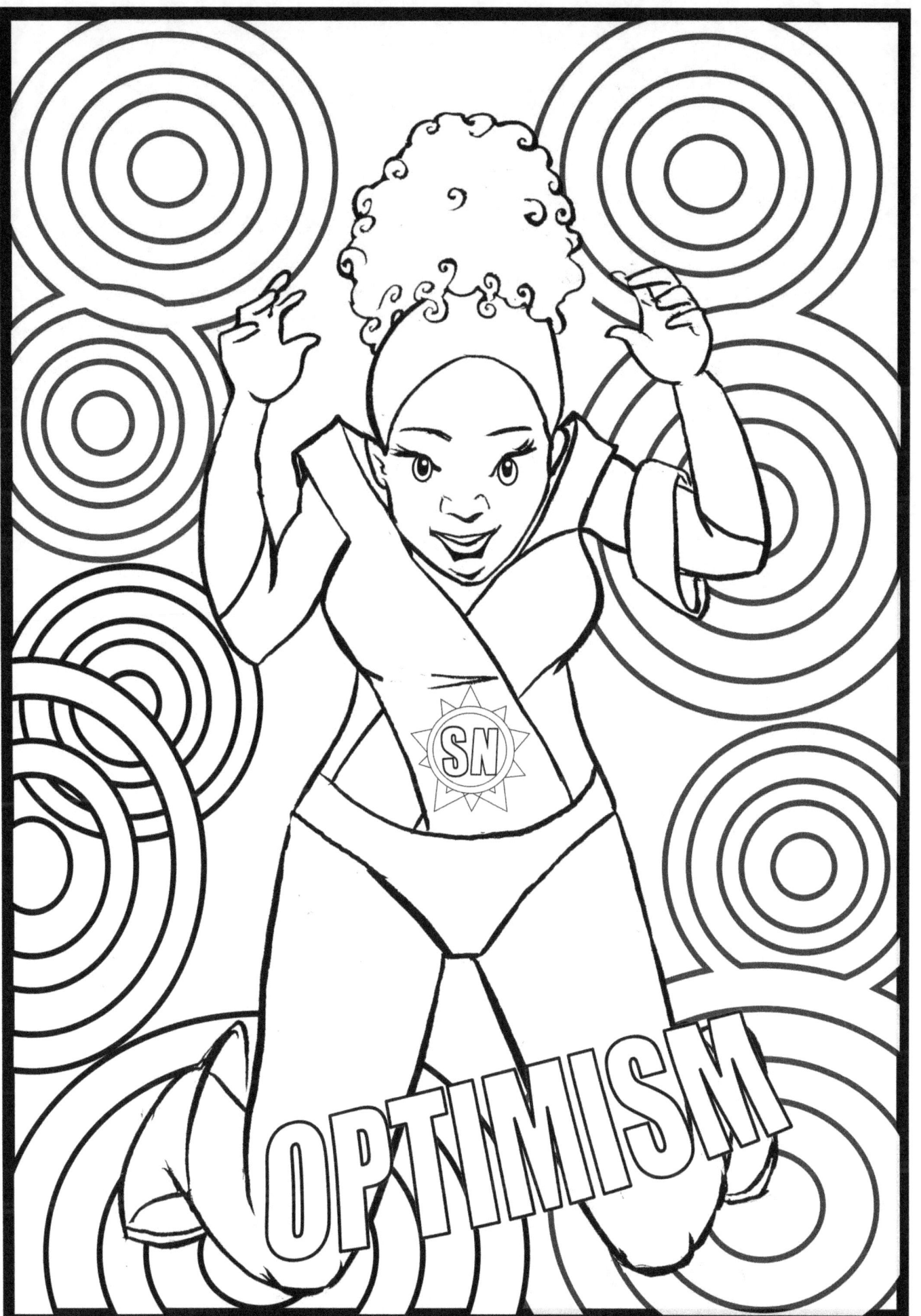

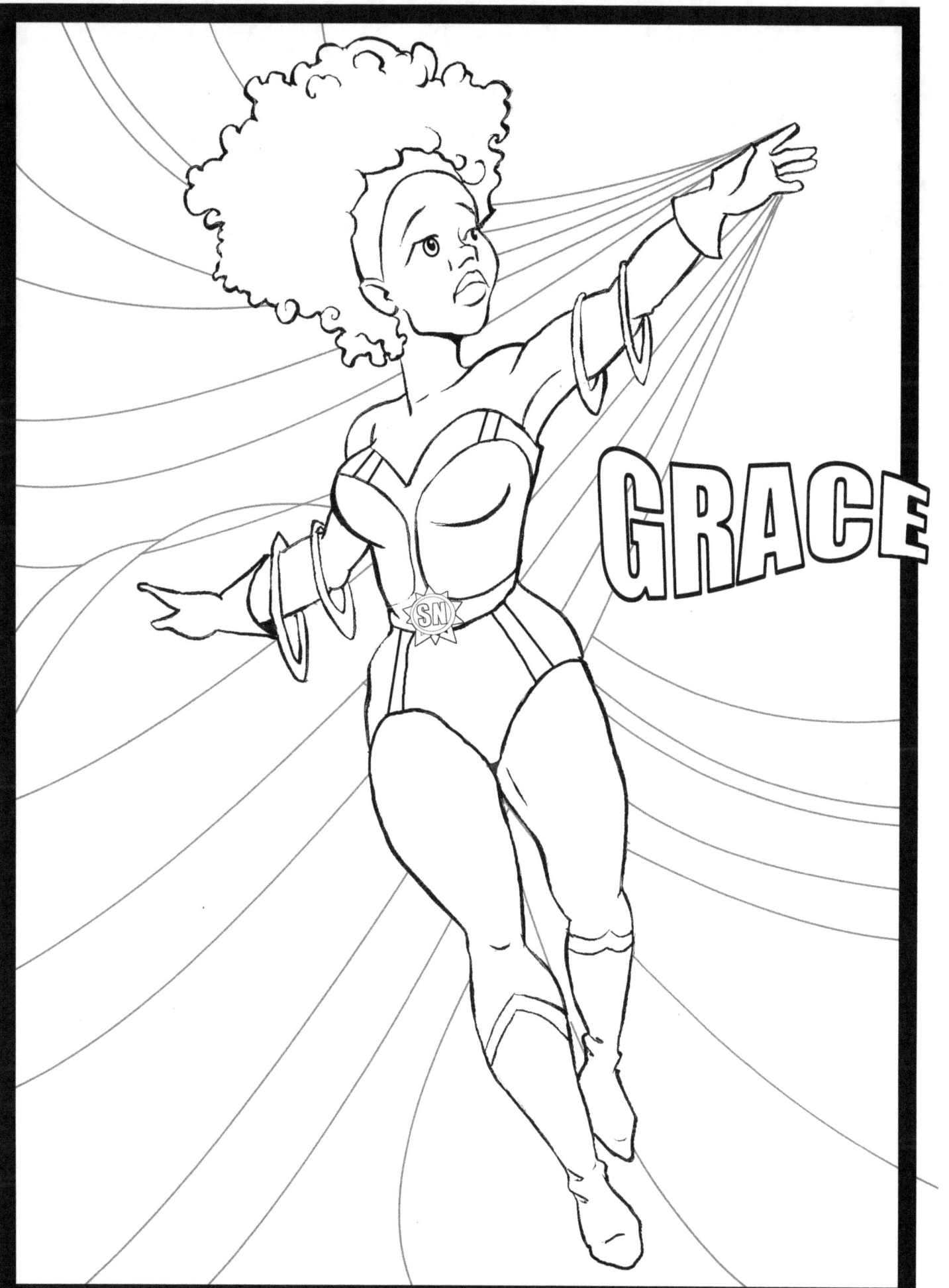

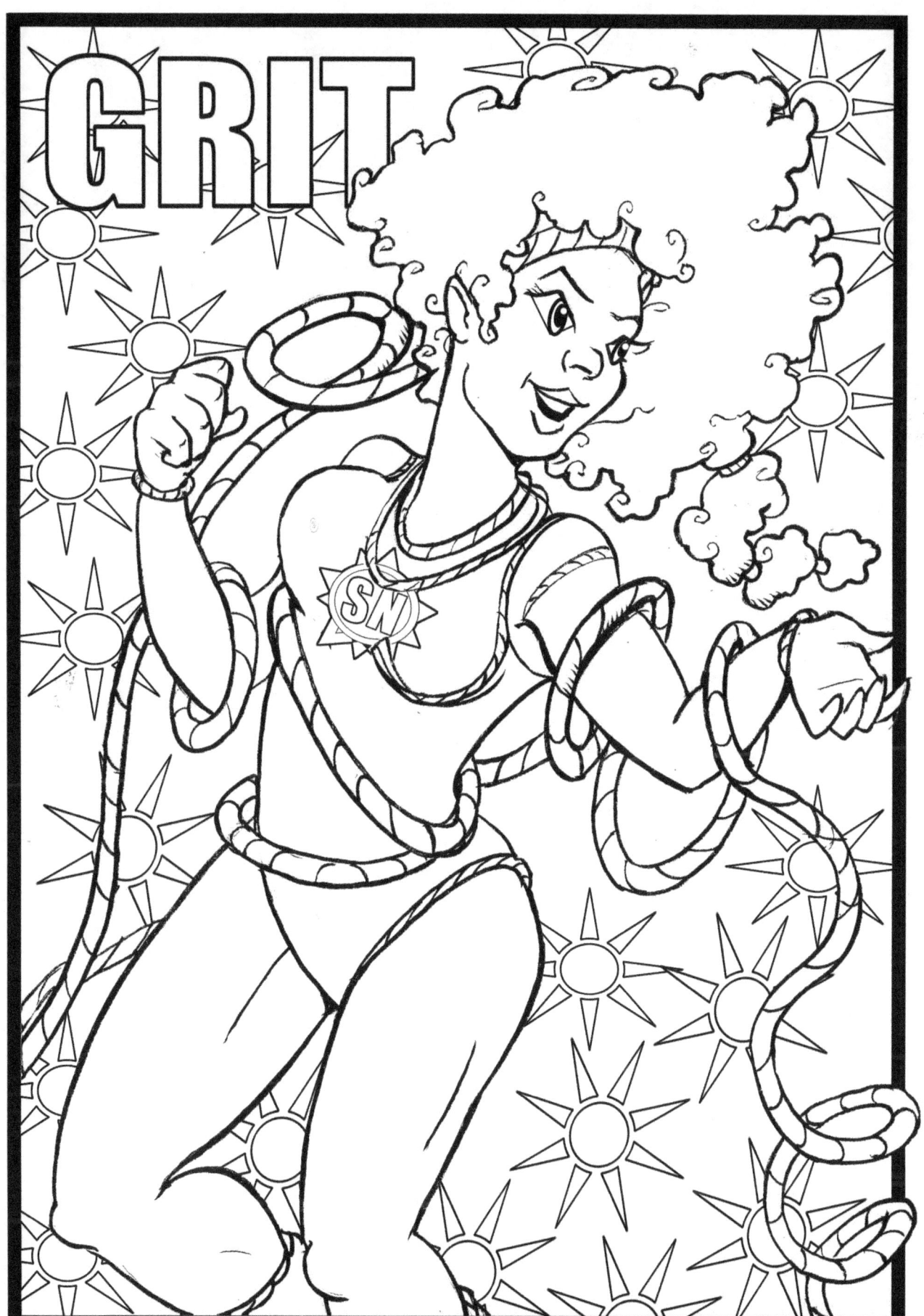

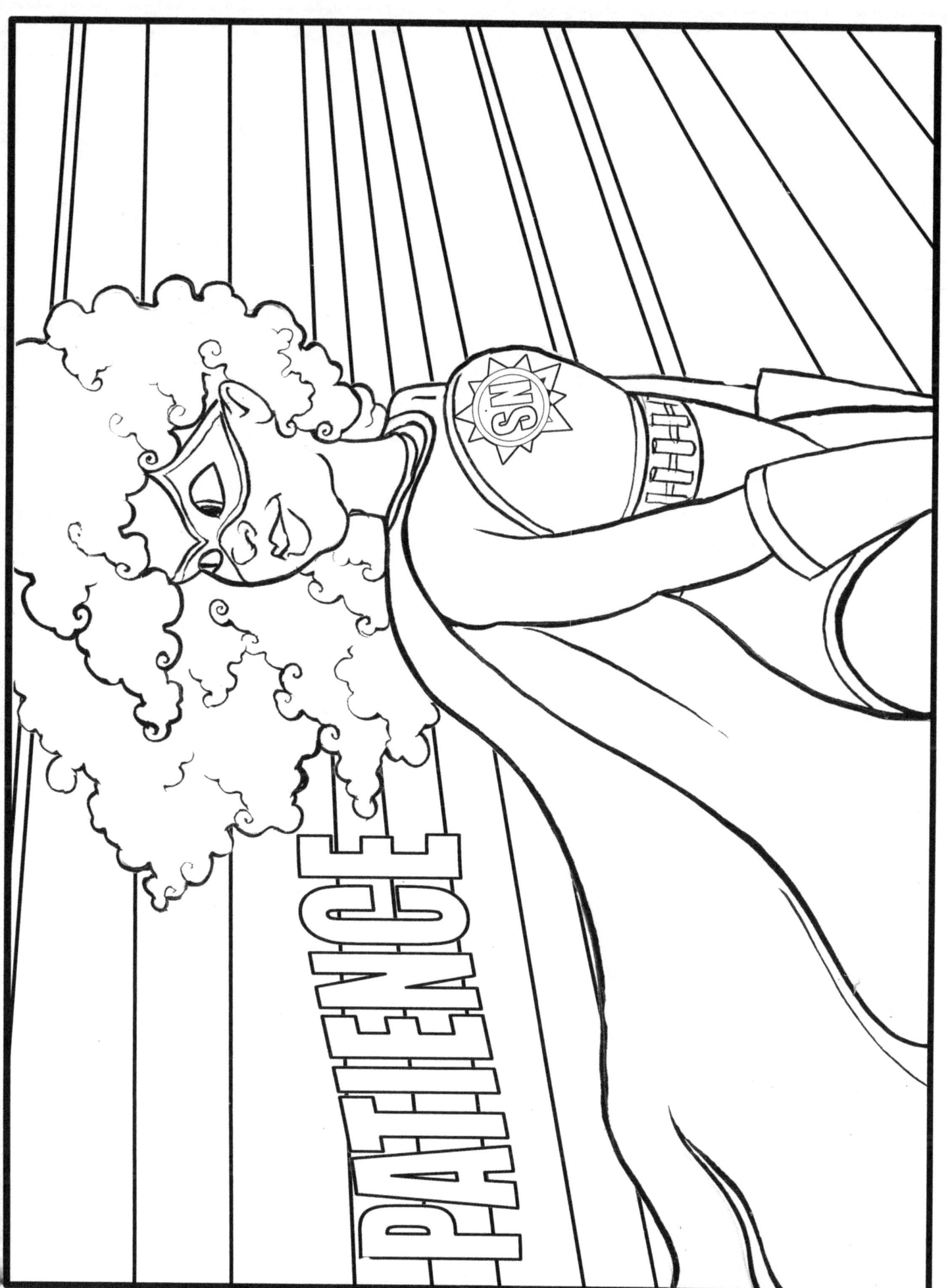

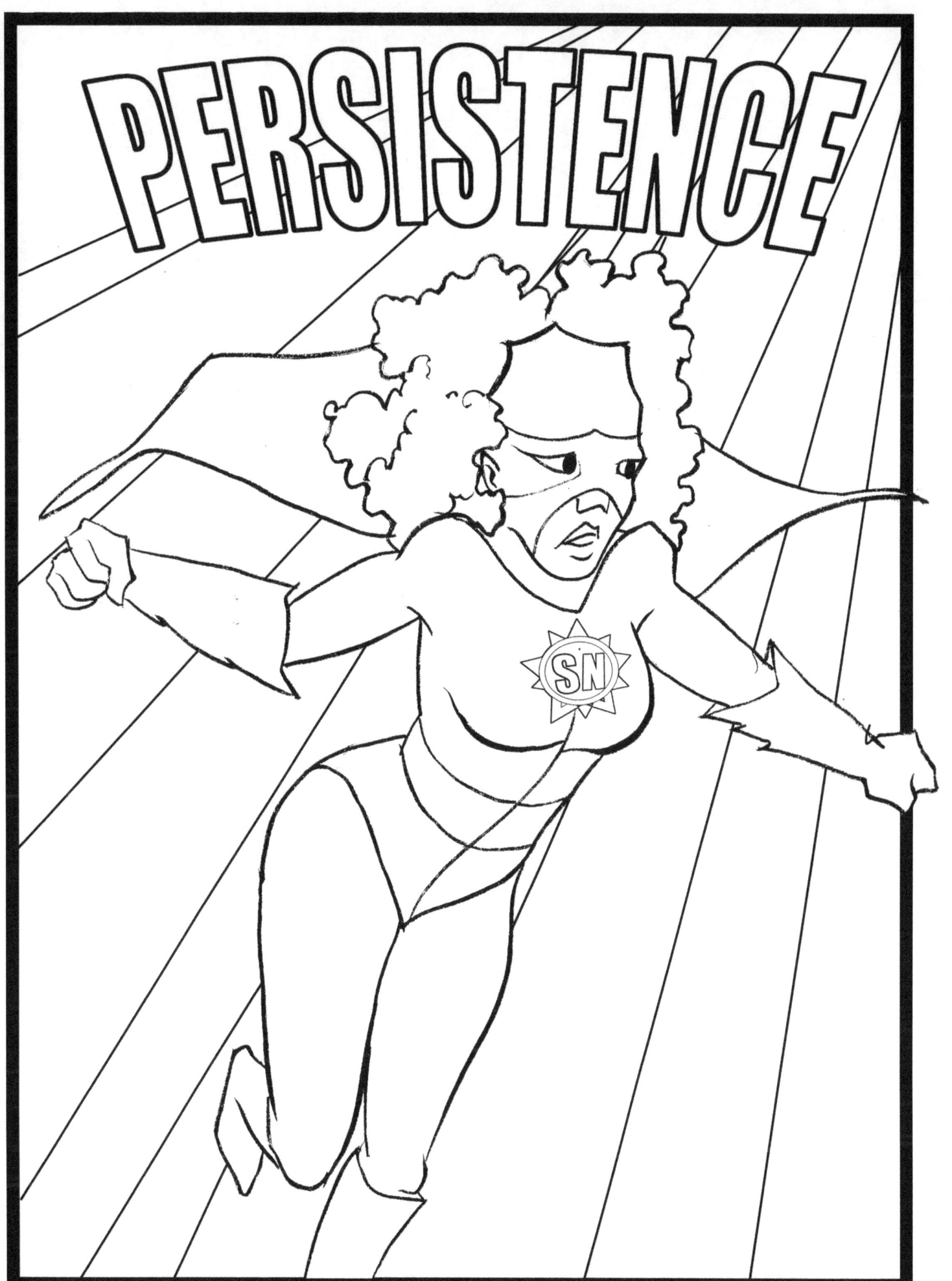

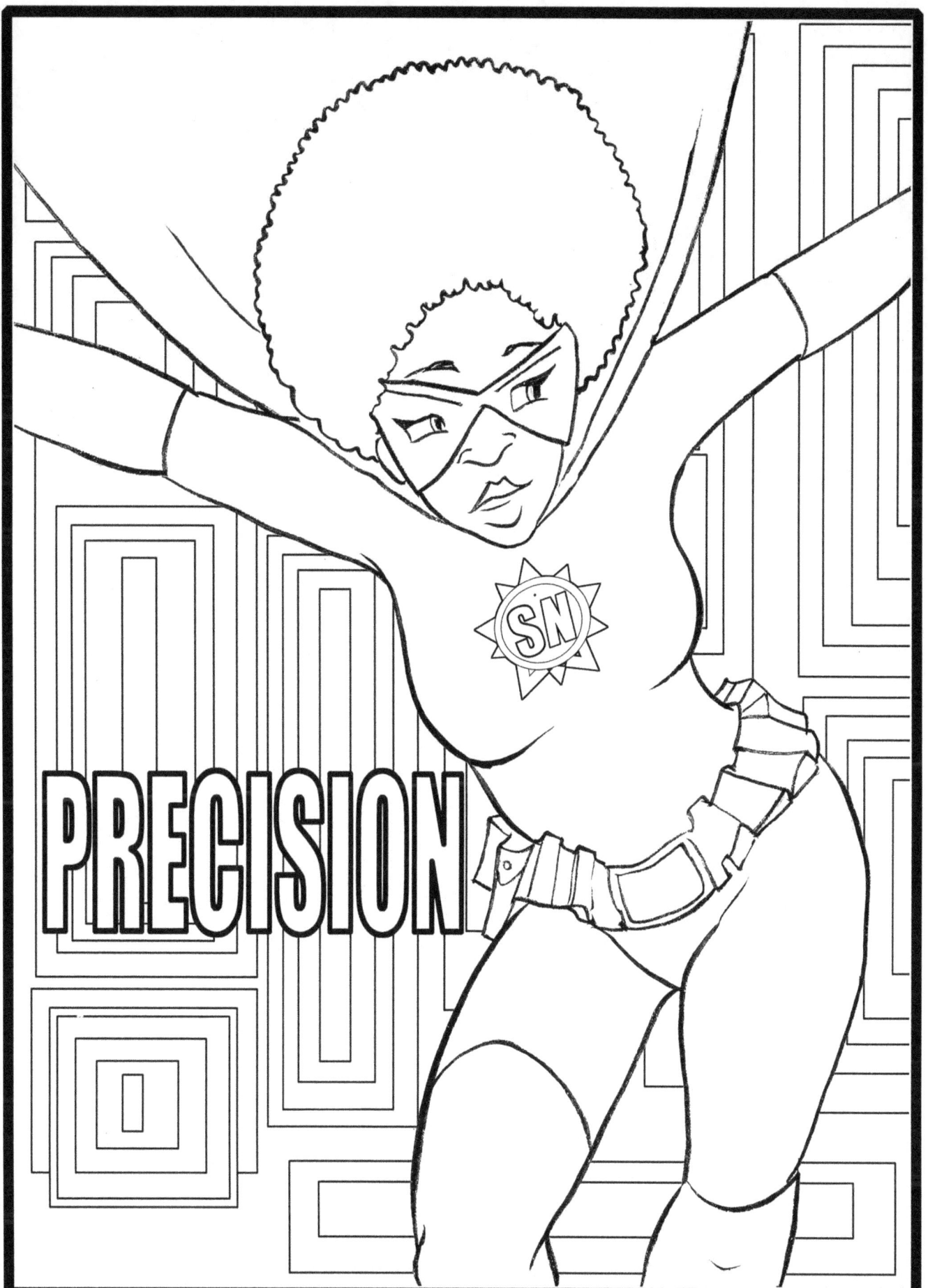

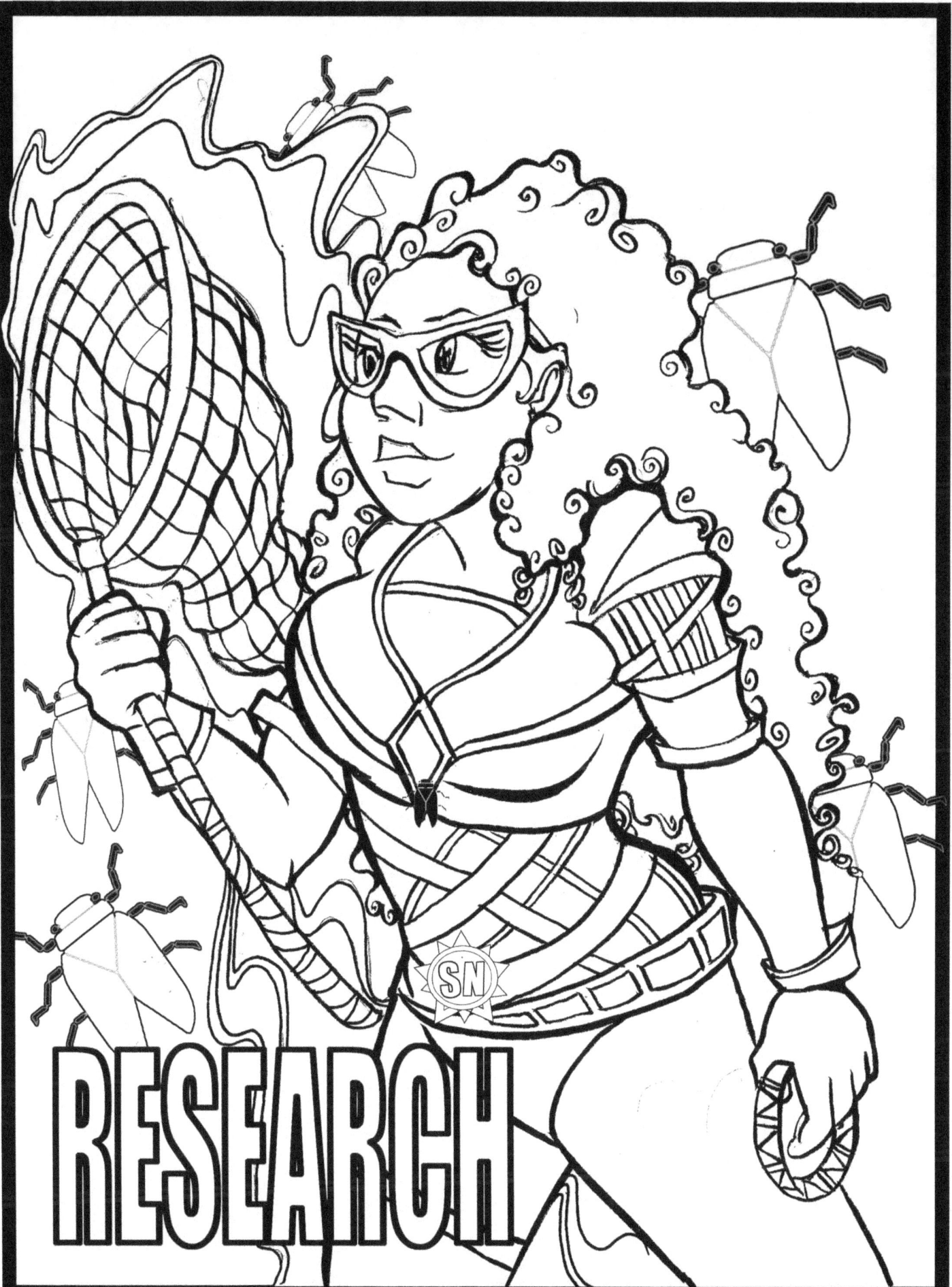

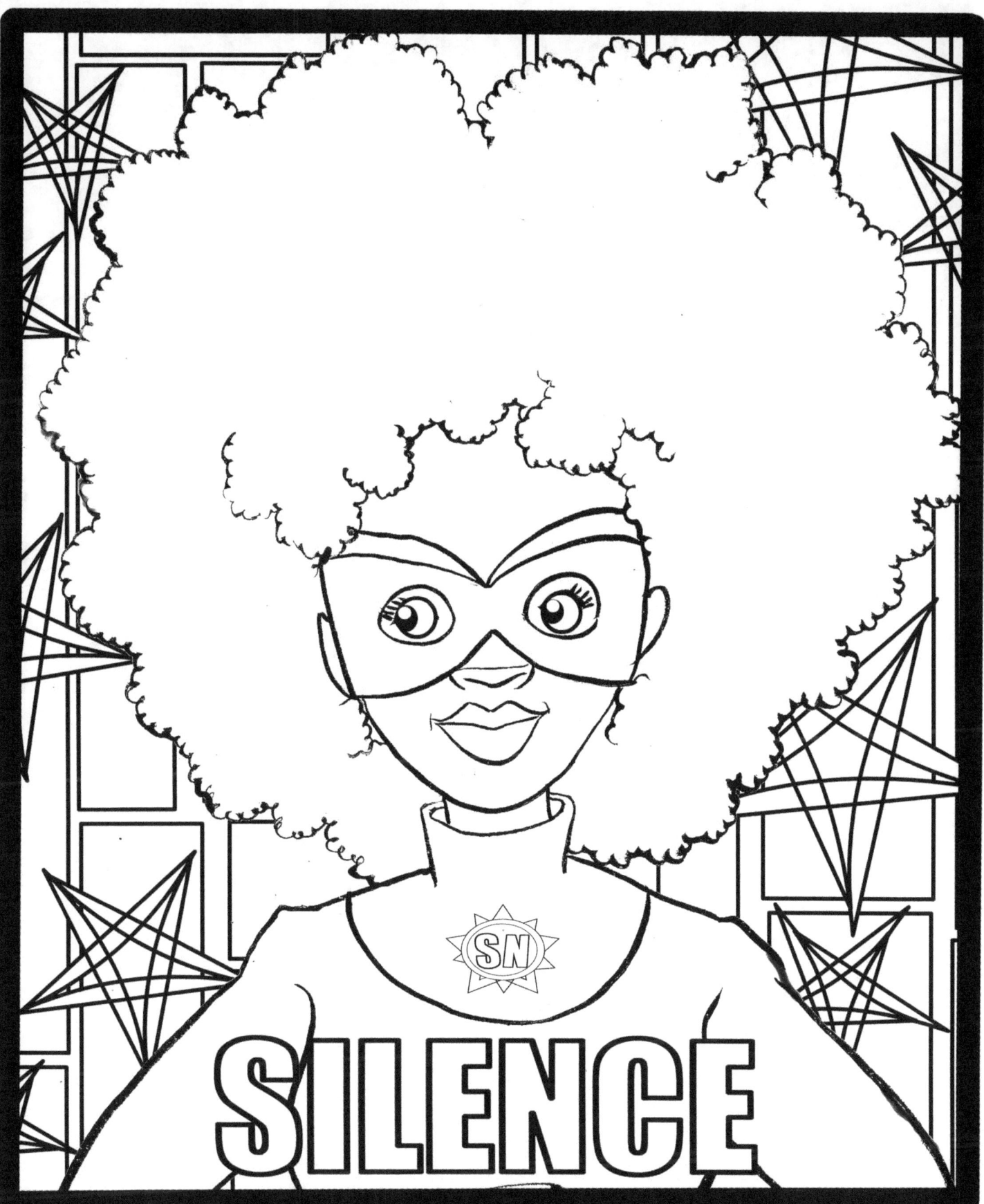

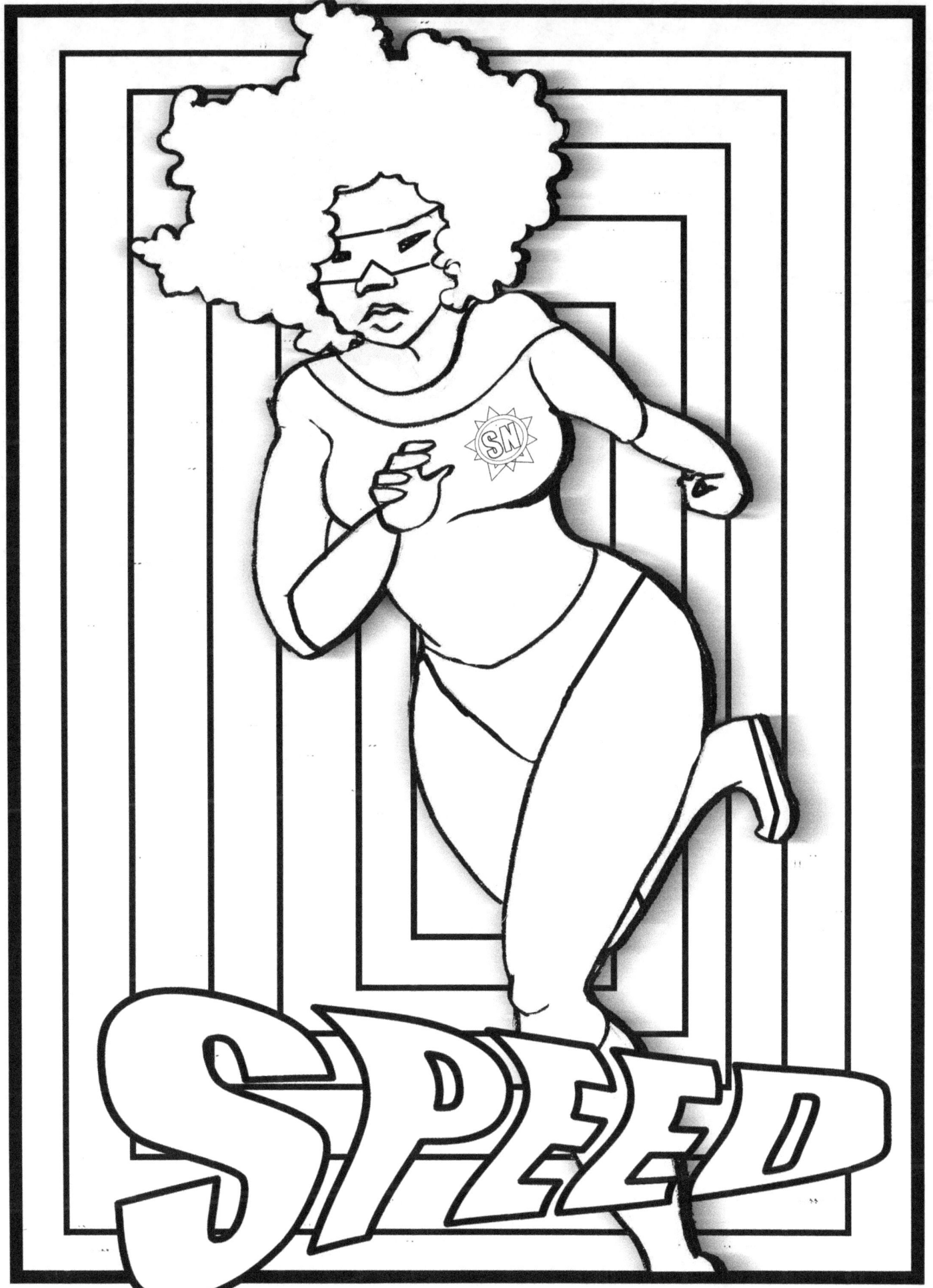

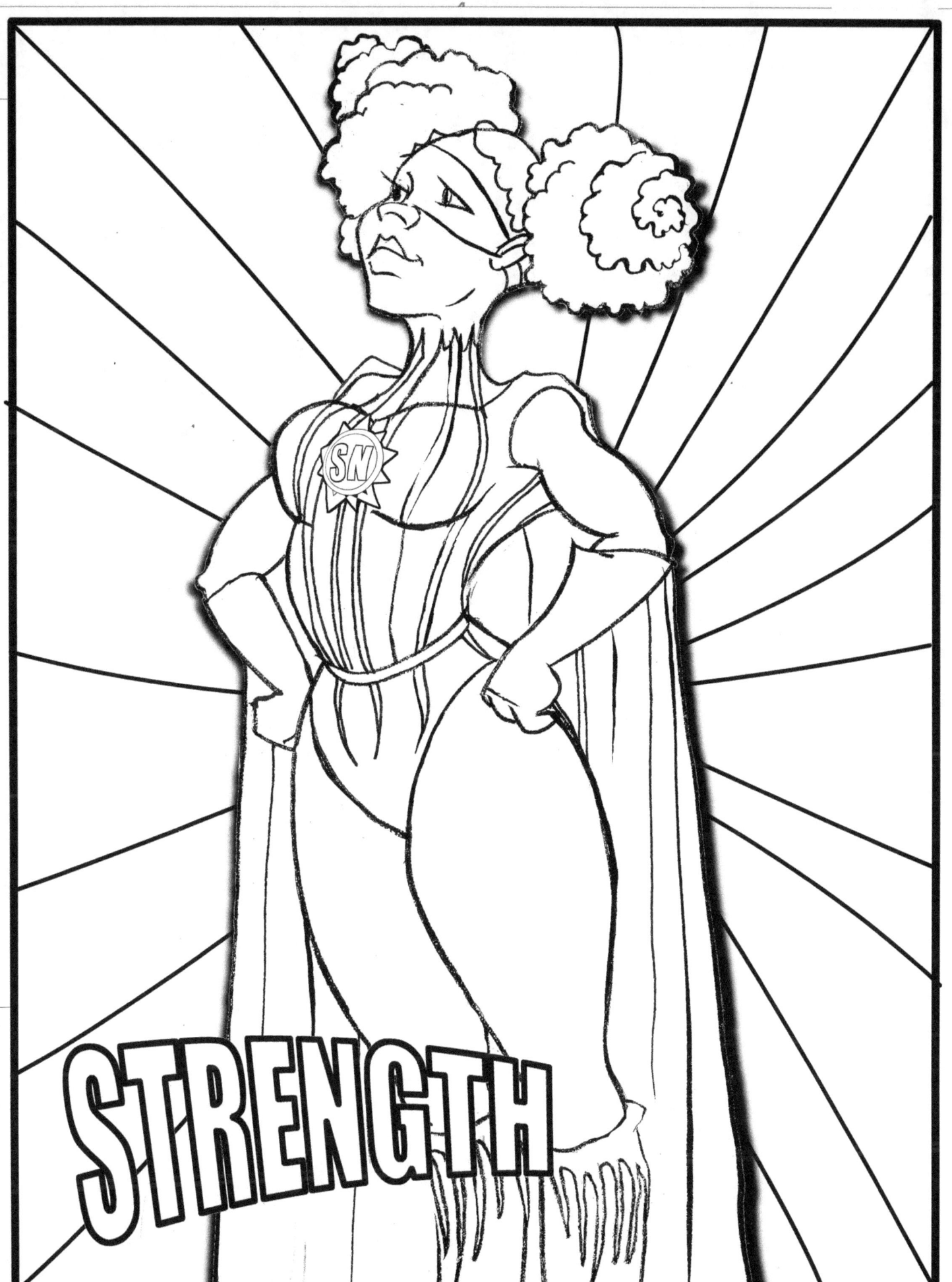

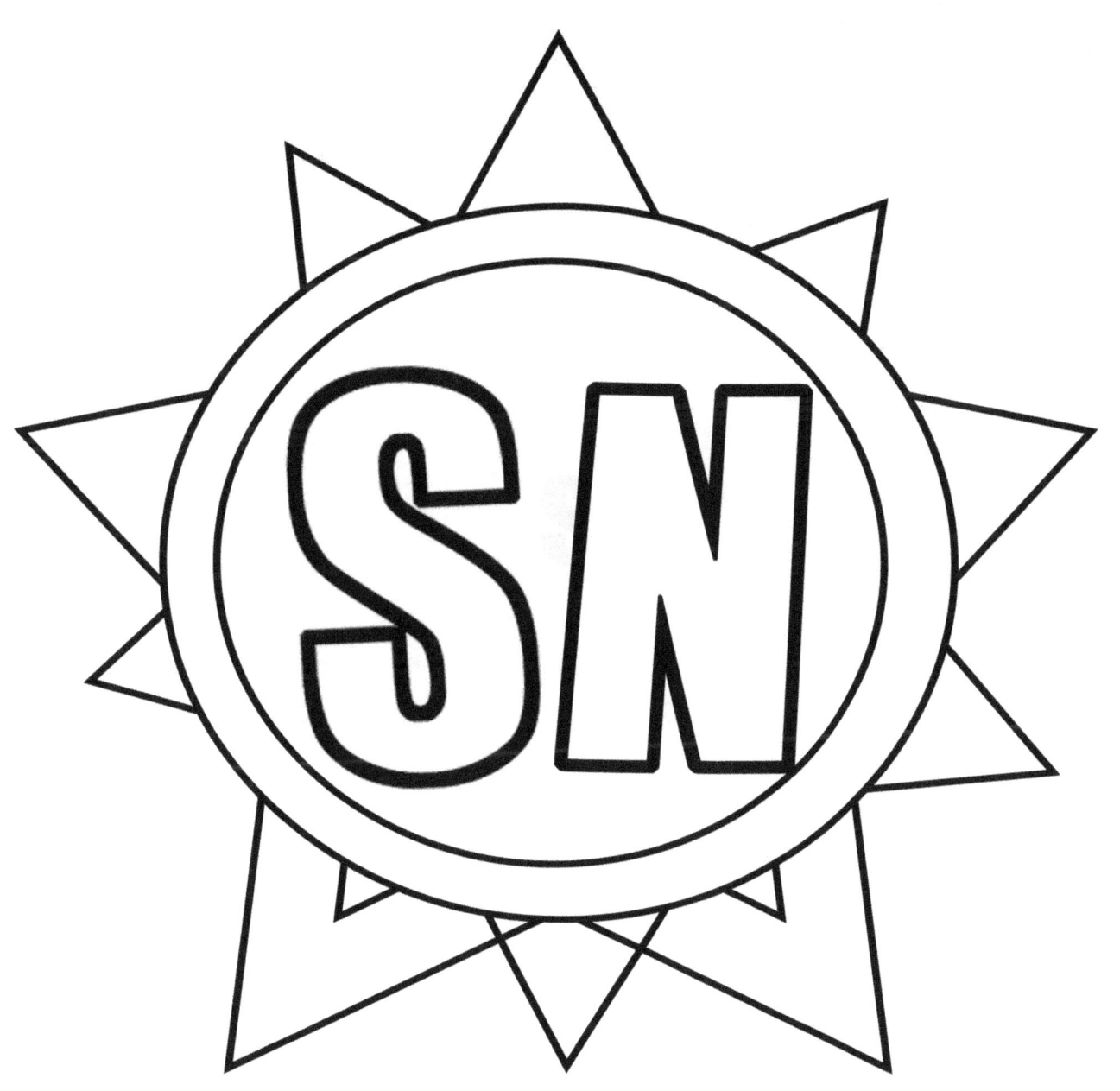

GREAT JOB!

We're one step closer
to saving the world. If
you know any other
superheroes that
can help write to
me at:

janine.carrington@gmail.com